SCHIRMER'S LIBRARY
OF MUSICAL CLASSICS

Vol. 898

The Little Pischna

Forty-Eight Practice-Pieces

For the Piano

Introduction to

Pischna's Sixty Progressive Exercises

Edited by

BERNHARD WOLFF

G. SCHIRMER, Inc.

DISTRIBUTED BY

HAL•LEONARD®
CORPORATION

7777 W. BLUEMOUND RD. P.O. BOX 13819 MILWAUKEE, WI 53213

The Little Pischna*

Johann Pischna
Edited by Bernhard Wolff

* So-called because written as an introduction to Pischna's more advanced "60 Exercises"

Moderato

Each measure 4 times

Moderato

Moderato
Each measure twice

13

f sempre legato

Moderato

14

f sempre legato

Moderato
Each measure twice

19

12

Moderato

Each measure twice

Moderato

Each measure twice

Moderato

36

f sempre legato

8 times

Moderato
Each measure twice

Moderato
Each measure twice

40

f sempre legato

41

Moderato

f sempre legato

4 times

*The fingering shown in brackets is to be used when the scales are practised consecutively

Moderato

42

f sempre legato

4 times

* The fingering shown in brackets is to be used when the scales are practised consecutively

*The fingering shown in brackets is to be used when the scales are practised **consecutively**

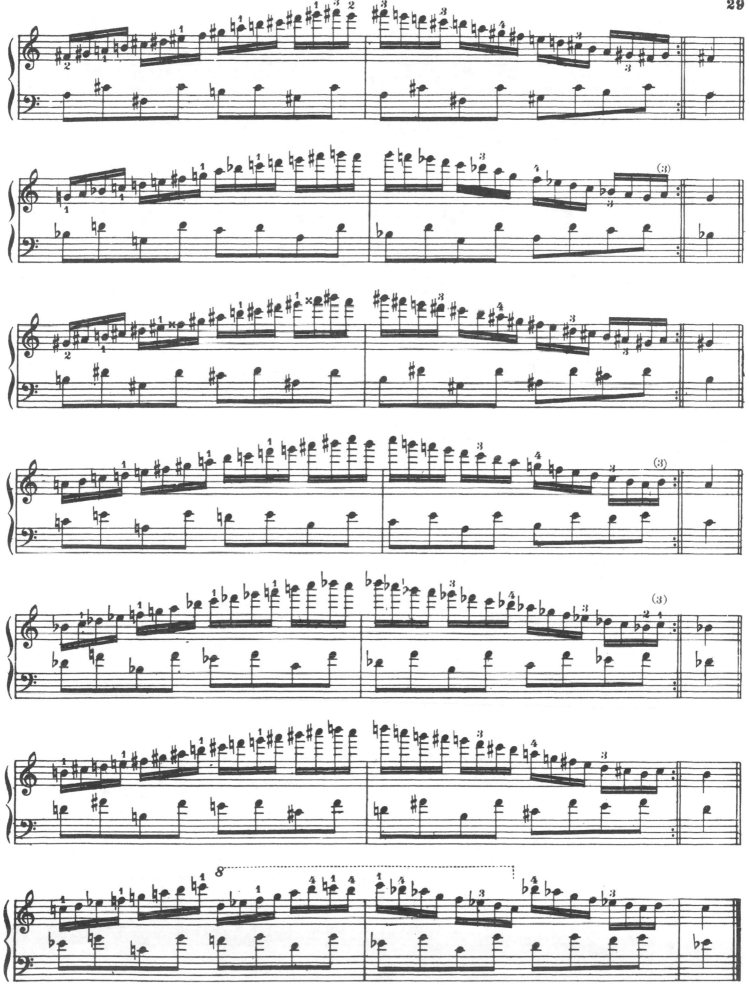

* The fingering shown in brackets is to be used when the scales are practised consecutively

Moderato

Moderato

46

Moderato

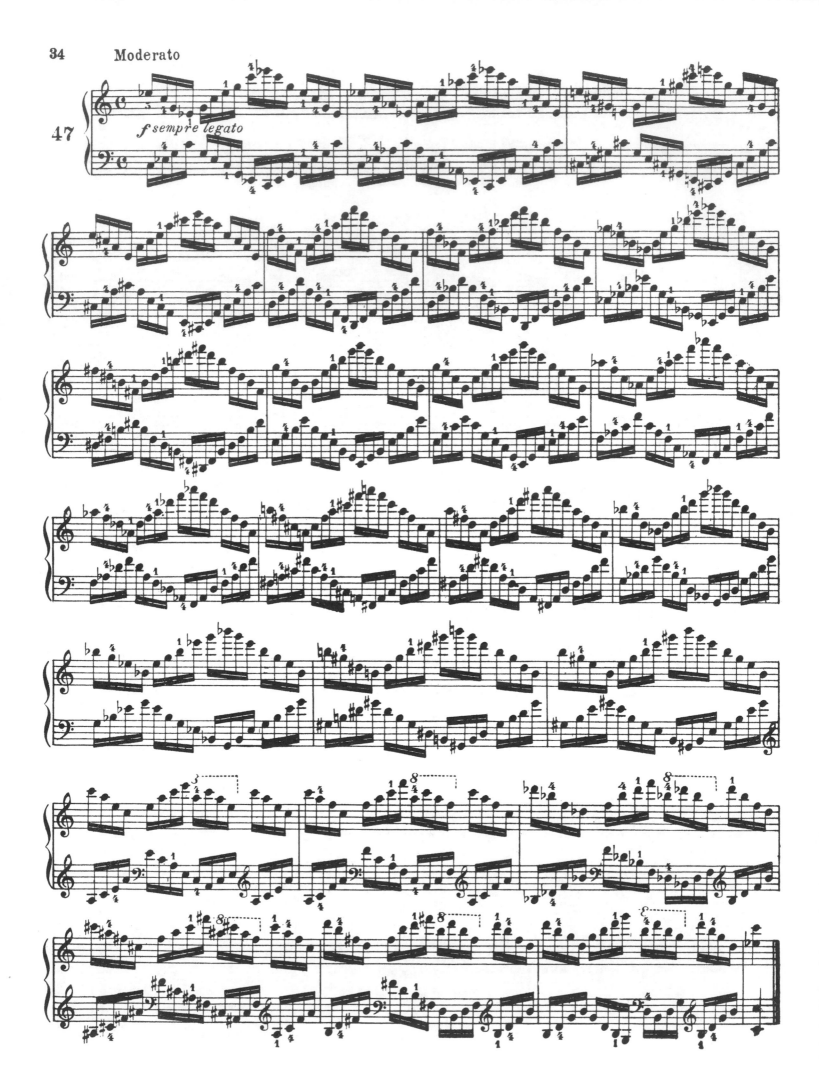

Scales

(a) Major Scales

(b) Melodic Minor Scales

Left hand an octave lower

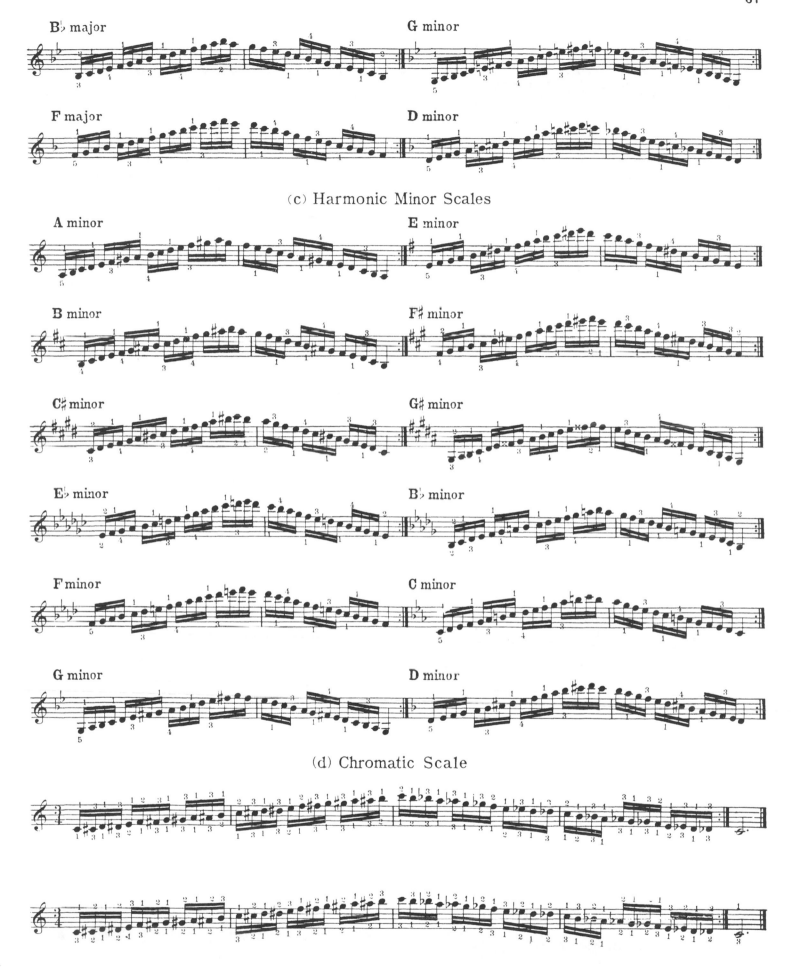

(c) Harmonic Minor Scales

(d) Chromatic Scale

Scales in Thirds

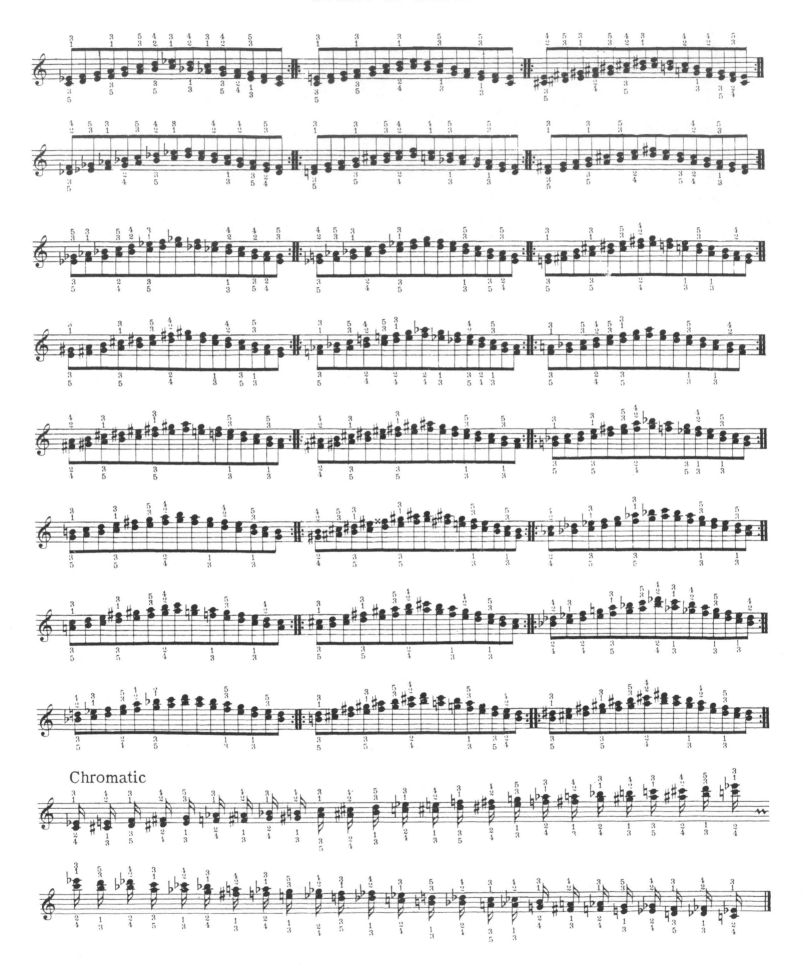

Chromatic